HEARTSEASE

Poems and Photographs
by Peter J Sisam

First published 2001
by Peter J Sisam
3 Henley Road
Marlow, Bucks
SL7 2BZ

ISBN: 0-9521865-1-97

Designed by Blair Cummock
Printed by Kelso Graphics, Kelso, Scotland

CONTENTS

Foreword	5
Journey North through Shap Fell	7
Sheffield Steel 1950	9
The Valley of the Windrush	10
June Rain	11
Summertime at Bourton	13
The Fosse Way at Moreton	16
Shakespeare's Avon	18
Exmoor	20
On giving a book to a younger Sister	22
Midnight in Mayfair	23
The Power to Move	24
On Crossing Brunel's Bridge	27
Pre-Dawn	28
London under Threat	29
Air raid on Good Friday	30
Tom Shillington	31
Into Europe, 1946	32
House upon the Mountain	34
Passion Elemental	36
Love and Truth	38
California	40
Stranger Rain	42
Hollywood Nocturne	44
Down-town Los Angeles	46
Thoughts of Africa	47
The Presence	48
Instruments	50
Early Morning in Hyde Park	52
Instant of Spring	54
Easter	57
July Bounty	55
Approach of Winter	
Yellow-gold	60
To Be	62
Homecoming	63
Delight	65
Tasks Completed	66
Notes on the poems	70

FOREWORD

According to tradition, the wildflower, Heartsease, has two associations. One is with fond memories, the other is with falling in love, as Shakespeare merrily portrays in his 'Midsummer Night's Dream'. Both these themes will be found in this book. I have chosen 'Heartsease' as its title because most of the poems have a heart-quality.

I make no claim to poetic genius, but I hope that in this collection there is something for everyone. Some may find what might be called jingles, others, examples of 'poetic prose', or a change of rhythm within a poem to reflect a change of mood. All I can say is that the poems are an honest expression of personal experience over sixty years. The diction is my own, and comes from reading, and some of it perhaps from a Cotswold background.

But, diction aside, to be able to share with others what has given me both happiness and food for thought, is in any case a joy.

PJS

JOURNEY NORTH THROUGH SHAP FELL

Train and shadow race together
In the morning sun,
Dancing over fern and heather
On the northern run.

Early hearth-smoke columns upward
In the stilly air;
Rabbits frisk upon the green-sward,
Gentle cattle stare.

Willow-herb and meadowsweet
Don their glad array;
Green fields lie in patterns neat,
Swathed in new-mown hay.

Crimson ramblers ring a porch,
Honeysuckles climb,
Flowers like a burning torch
Shed a glow sublime.

Footpath leading to a stile
Marks the glowing green,
Grass as thick as carpet pile,
Tipped with dewy sheen.

O to be in upland pasture,
Where the great clouds rest
Silent in the realms of nature,
Where the lapwings nest.

There the heart is sifted soon,
And the will set free,
Listening in the still of noon
To eternity.

SHEFFIELD STEEL
1950

Viewed atop the swaying bus,
Climbing from the Moor,
This city of the River Don
O'erflows the valley floor,
Where men of skill and courage kneel
In homage to the molten steel,
And quiet flows the Don.

In evening when the sun is low,
From every smoking stack
Thick incense rises to the sky,
Brown and white and black,
Where men of strength and purpose toil
To forge the precious, molten spoil,
And swiftly flows the Don.

As the darkness swallows up
The foundries and the smoke
All else is silent now except
The hammer's heavy stroke,
While furnaces to left and right
Reveal the labour through the night,
And darkly flows the Don.

White-hot metal, liquid, flowing
In the furnace-heart;
White-hot passion, molten growing
In the human heart,
Both eager to full-brim the mould,
Reshaping new worlds from the old,
As fiercely flows the Don.

THE VALLEY OF THE WINDRUSH AT NAUNTON

When I take the upland road
That bounds across this windswept wold,
I shout and sing for joy that I
Was born and bred of Cotswold mould.

As the way runs on and on
There is a valley comes to view,
With dwellings clustered here and there
Of weathered stone and lichened hue,

In whose gardens beehives stand,
With flowers planted in between,
And by their walls the Windrush goes,
Flowing on to meadows green.

Look onward whence the waters come,
Hid in the depths of wood and hill,
A holy spot and place of peace,
With power to strengthen heart and will.

JUNE RAIN
NEAR LONGBOROUGH

When rain falls on these hilltops
And sweeps across the vale,
And storm-cloud, swoln with raindrops,
Empties out its sail,
The Cotswold rain comes falling
Across the grey-stone walling,
An honest, steady rain,
'Till waters flow again,
And every brook and rill
Goes singing down the hill.

Descending from these ridges,
Trees wrapt in liquid mist,
Stand out above the hedges
Like ships by storm-seas kissed.
But when the rain is still
And silence shrouds each hill,
The sun at last breaks free,
Sparkling earth and tree.
Then hill and vale rejoice,
And blackbird adds his voice.

SUMMERTIME AT BOURTON–ON–THE–HILL

In Bourton Wood the hot sun falls
Through leafy roof of arching trees,
That line the long low mellow walls
And fashion dappled canopies.

High above, the white clouds ride,
Majestic masses in the blue,
Sailing on an aerial tide,
From Broadway Tower to Little Tew.

In Bourton village all is still
About the cool and ancient stone,
Fashioned by a loving skill,
But with a beauty of its own.

Here mullioned windows yet survey
Aubretia in a well-kept bed,
With hollyhocks in rich array,
And lavender with roses red;

While all around the church's tower
The forebears of the village sleep,
Content that here within this bower
Some still the olden customs keep.

THE FOSSE WAY AT MORETON 1934

Straight as an arrow's flight, the Roman Road
Runs on and on through this last Cotswold town,
Where, darting from the limestone hills, it seeks
The undulating ways of Warwickshire.

At first approach the town is unpretentious:
A wayside inn that welcomed travellers,
A horse-pool, where their hard-worked steeds
Would snort and stamp and slake their thirst.

But at this spot the Roman Way expands
To march majestically in broad estate,
By avenue of trees, where busy sounds
Of trade amidst old houses fills the air.

Here rings the tinkling, bouncing shoe-shop bell
At Mrs Lamb's. To hand is saddler Juffs,
And opposite is stout old Mrs Pitts,
Presiding at her fizzing Vimto fount;

There, Percy Strong and Harry, busy both
With tweeds and breeches, Burberrys, suits bespoke.
Nearby, fishmonger Price is cool amidst his ice,
(But standing at the wicket cooler still);

There's Willy Tarplett, whistling door-to-door
With gleaming pail of milk and shining scoop;
And willing Tommy Walker, ever there,
Ready to trundle baggage to the train;

Percy Sheen, ironmonger, housewives' friend,
With garage, buses, petrol, cars to hire;
And Raymond Gleed, watchmaker, jeweller, radio man,
Courageous, cheerful ever, yet though lifelong lame;

Then jovial family butcher, Charlie Drury,
Skilled carver at the Moreton ox-roast fair,
And brother Arthur, deep in town affairs,
A stalwart pillar of the hospital;

Smiling Tommy Payne, the postmaster,
Directing mails on weekdays next the inn,
Who every Sunday, clad in verger's robe,
So faithfully welcomes worshippers to church.

Midtown still keeps its ancient curfew tower,
Once rung to summon forth the fire brigade;
Whilst opposite, a hostelry stands proud
For having welcomed here an English king.

Across the road, to Foden's, ladies go,
Where William Spearing, business-like and brisk,
'Midst blouses, ribbons, frocks and hats galore,
Meets every fancy whim with patient smile.

By the Town Hall, Joe Smith, the chemist lives,
The friend of all, provider of the dose
That soothes the tum, or syrup for a cough,
Who takes your films and hands them back as snaps.

A few doors down Joe Emes cuts hair for boys
At only fourpence each, and offers choice
Of multitudinous Meccano parts
To lucky ones with any pence to spare.

The family Horne have served this town through trade
And school and hospital – none have done more.
Andrew Horne's grand grocery store stands next
The Riddeys' fine, imposing up-down 'Steps'.

Beyond them lives his uncle, farmer Leo,
Radical, public-spirited, sincere;
And there goes Doctor Nicholson, the Scot,
Returning to his home at town's far end;

Where now the Roman Way at last takes leave
Of all these folk, whose history past and present
Of hopes, endeavours, joys and sorrows are
Encapsulated in this single street.

For here the Roman Road now sets it's course
To golden Lincoln, standing tall and strong,
As guardian of those other, northern wolds,
The Wolds of Lincolnshire.

SHAKESPEARE'S AVON

By wooded banks the flowing stream
Runs on to meadowed bowers,
With may and marybuds agleam
And dainty cuckoo-flowers.

Now ponderous, slow and rhythmical,
Now rippling through the narrows,
It twists in shapes symetrical
Through deeps and pebbled shallows.

Coursing down the willowed curve,
It shoots through many an arch,
To where, in elm-girt silence, sleeps
The poet-patriarch.

Then, gliding by the slender spire
In broadening contemplation,
It plunges headlong down the weir
In thunderous salutation.

EXMOOR

We took the sheep-track from the water,
Climbing to the moor,
Our footsteps sunk in yielding heather
On the earthen floor.

The bracken fronds were browner
Since we passed a week ago,
Their lacey patterns glinting crisply
In the evening's glow.

We walked beneath a changing sky,
Decked with wisps of gold,
Urging us to speed our steps,
Towards the distant fold.

Vein-like hedges up and down,
Marked the nearing fields of Oare,
Above them stacks of jet-black peat
Stood outlined on the moor.

At last the final rise was won.
Ahead the coast of Wales lay,
Her mountains standing timelessly,
Watchmen of departing day.

ON GIVING A BOOK TO A YOUNGER SISTER

Mental strivings,
Hurried scribblings,
Brilliant flashes,
Blots and dashes,
Midnight oil,
Daylight toil,
Of such things are books conceived.

Shining covers,
Tales of lovers,
Gilded edges,
Broken pledges,
Expectations,
Recollections,
Of such things are books contrived.

Peace and strife,
Death and life,
Joy and gladness,
Mingled sadness,
Hopes and visions,
Hard decisions,
From such things experience grows.

Childhood's parting,
Future's starting.
Learn from books
How life looks.
Love of living,
Selfless giving,
Of such things is life composed.

MIDNIGHT IN MAYFAIR

The office door is closed behind
And lights are out. The very air hangs still,
The street is clothed in silver mist.
The lines of chimney-pots stand out like battlements,
With details blurred, and underneath the moon
The whole takes on a beauty that in daylight is unknown.

Crewe House gleams white in Curzon Street,
It's sentry trees marked clear against the sky.
A solitary taxi picks its way in search of fares.
The commissionaire at Shepherd's, long since closed,
Has left his post beside the empty kerb.
A crack of light shines from a nightclub door;

Within, slow drawl and rhythmic beat
Mask apathy and languid hearts.
How neat the shining cobble-stones appear,
As row on row they glisten to the constant moon,
Their antique permanence reproving us
For empty shallowness in much of what we do.

The day has lasted long,
'Tis good to turn the key
And know that sleep awaits.
Tomorrow we will rise refreshed
To work with renewed hope
For the world that is to be.

THE POWER TO MOVE

The rise and fall of distant bells,
Ships on a silver sea,
Big Ben that every hour tells,
Singers in harmony;

Pale winter sunlight, yellow-red,
Full foliage of June,
Lark's song thrilling overhead,
Clouds riding high at noon;

The murmur of the honey-bees,
Hot sunlight on the skin,
Space glimpsed upward through the trees,
Grasshoppers' drowsy din;

Engine's surge through jet-black night,
Crescendo peak of gears,
The electricity of touch,
The pent-up power of tears;

These speak.

ON CROSSING BRUNEL'S BRIDGE AT SALTASH

July 1938

Are we worthy of the glory of this Land,
Of golden sun and rolling hills,
Of woods and slopes, of green and watered dells?
Have we not valued selfish, hard desires
Above the needs of this our precious home?

O that there might burn in us refining fire
To match this fateful, dangerous hour
As Europe trembles on the brink of war,
And nations choose, like us, what suits them best,
Rather than the rougher path of right.

Such fire could fast consume the lesser flames,
That fade because they spring from self.
There might then be a giving that for all
Renounces all, a spirit pure and strong,
Born of decisions of the heart and will.

Can we make that decision now,
And cross the crucial bridge?
If then the fire of war should come,
Dedicated hearts will form a bedrock firm,
On which in years to come to build a safer, saner world.

PRE-DAWN

How still the rounded moon
Hangs now against the starry dome,
How still the patterned trees
Now hold their tracery on high,
How still the city lies.

This is the precious hour,
When to men's minds attuned
God's wisdom is instilled,
And human will recedes in awe
Before a greater one.

The two when joined may then
Release a powerful healing
To a starved and weary world,
Compassion rare, bold truth,
And wondrous new creation.

LONDON UNDER THREAT
June 1940

This is the night
Of stars and soft June air,
When hell was to be rained
Upon these streets and squares.

Is it then true
That we have been reprieved
An hour, a day, perhaps,
A week, or even more?

Impossible it seems
That these same streets,
So neat, may in a trice
Become a desolation.

We live now by the hour,
Going about our tasks,
Silent, with no time to speak
Our deepest thoughts,
For they have scarcely formed.
Far better to be busy
Than to chatter idly on.

In the silence there is strength,
From therein springs the rock-based faith,
Through which all terrors and eventualities
Can be faced, and dear friends comforted.

AIR RAID ON GOOD FRIDAY

April 11, 1941

Three o'clock, the dawn is distant yet.
The April moon rides clear above the roofs,
Constant, unlike the broken silences
Between the thunder of the Hyde Park guns;
'And it was the third hour and they crucified him'.

Comes a droning aircraft from the east.
All hell's let loose by anti-aircraft guns.
A million fragments burst about the sky,
As Hyde Park answers Hampstead to and fro.
The windows rattle, settle and lie still.

This Friday morn death stalks across the earth,
As over nineteen hundred years ago
A blind and hating crowd with twisted mind
Made liberty and justice but a mockery,
That Friday morn when hope was put to death.

This April morning nineteen forty-one
The radio spans the surface of the earth:
Music from Stuttgart, news in Greek, Italian, French;
Melodic voices joined in Easter hymn;
'And it was the third hour and they crucified him.'

TOM SHILLINGTON

Who died in the Battle of El Alamein

He was a veteran fighter,
Seasoned by daily combat,
In the fight to build a world
Where greed should be no more,

Not ingloriously he fell,
But riding forth triumphant into battle,
Irish and blithe across the Libyan sands;
Knowing that every battle can be won.

Then suddenly the stillness came,
As deep as on this wintry morn
Now lies upon these moon-washed roofs,
These roofs he knew so well.

He died that we might live
To build a world on which
Millions set their hearts;
And he is with us now,
Comrade once on earth,
And comrade still in heaven.

INTO EUROPE – 1946

"All's well. in England",
So seems the clock to say at Waterloo
As travellers take their seats
For Paris, Engadine and Rome.
Yet, very soon these trains may stand inert
For lack of coal, and homely hearths
Shelter only shivering ones.

"Now Calais is at peace",
So says the evening sun that spreads its gold
Across the waiting Paris train.
Soon the cautious engine picks its way
Through battle-scarred Boulogne, shattered
And boulder-strewn; then past Amiens,
Its fields bereft of milking cows.

"Is butter rationed still?"
Inquires the woman in the white-clothed dining car,
Between the glasses of vermouth
And claret red. Her boyfriend nods.
Four coaches on, the locomotive men,
Proud heroes of Resistance,
Labour and sweat in grimey cab,

To tend their streaming thunderbolt.
Such men as these had weeks before
Brought France near anarchy with strife.
Now she is fighting desperately
To save her life, as a committed few
Undermine and thwart the work
Of those who seek to save and heal.

Not all perceive the fight,
The people waiting now at quiet Mouchard,
Do any there perceive?
The corn stooks stand in early dew,
Precious gifts of nature's bounteous store,
Determinents of whether children shall
Go hungry through the winter's cold.

We pass, and then there comes
The frontier of Switzerland at last,
Where generous Swiss
With butter, rolls, black cherry jam,
Unrationed in this thrifty, peaceful land,
Bid welcome in their precious haven
To the weary-worn of Europe.

HOUSE UPON THE MOUNTAIN

Caux-sur-Montreux

Silent beneath the snows the house has lain
Throughout long winter months,
Germinating powerfully,
As the perennial narcissi
That white the meadows in the spring.

Now turrets, pinnacles and lofty rooms
Have come alive as hammers
Beat on wood, and steel saws sing.
Paint and plaster flow through willing hands,
And sun and spring invade the rooms.

To Mountain House, set high upon the slopes
Above the shining Lake,
Come men and women of affairs,
As in days long past they often came
To some blest spot on pilgrimage.

The road zig-zags athwart the mountain face,
As does the road of life,
Rough and steep at times, at others
Mild and smooth, but crowned at last,
With vistas of eternity.

Here clouded minds are cleansed of human dross,
Visions form and patterns shape,
For nations, and communities;
And individual destinies
Are glimpsed amidst the silent peaks.

PASSION ELEMENTAL

Col de Chaud, Villeneuve

Deliberate and unchanging as the centuries
Climbs the path towards the peak.
The sun has slanted through the trees a thousand years,
Making cross-patterns on the earth.
The mountain spring, filling the cupped hand,
Flows from the hollowed rock as did such streams
For men of Uri, Schwych and Unterwalden,
Six hundred years ago.

Tall overarching hazel, elder, sloe and ash,
Shape tunnels leading onwards,
Moss-lined, as if with emerald velvet, green and cool.
Above stand pines, with needle carpet
Spread beneath in patterned warp and woof
And over smooth-sawn stumps, placed here and there,
Like covered tables neatly laid with linen
Set for elfin feasts.

One further upward thrust, the climbing path
Bursts into a hidden, sunlit meadow,
Filled with ringing bells, where milk-kine graze content.
Below, the stately pines descend
In ordered lines between the timber slides.
Down these steep chutes the new-felled trunks resound,
Leaping, bouncing, with a boom like distant thunder,
While all else is still.

Far beyond, where placid waters of the lake
Lap the neighbouring shore of France,
Companion peaks stand wrapped in violent storm.
There, dark clouds mass in mighty column.
Thunder rolls. For miles the sky is veiled
In sombre curtain, moving fast across the vault
And lightning plays upon its darkening folds,
While thunder shakes the air.

The first drops fall, precursors of the flood
That sends the dry spouts gushing.
Yet passion quickly ebbs as clouds are loosed.
Beneath the sun the meadow lies,
A giant cauldron steaming and full-brimmed.
Now all is silent, save for that slow drip
From wooden spout, beneath a barn's roof-eave;
And peace is regnant now.

LOVE AND TRUTH

A walk from Slindon to Arundel

All living and green things that dwell on Sussex earth,
Beneath the kindly sun, bear witness of rebirth.

In April sun, beside the corner of a wood,
You turned and rent the mists of self-deceit,
Until truth shone and showed me what I was.

I, humbled and unarmed, loved you the more,
Sharp though the knife, and answer could I none.
Deeper the silence then, and wild creatures ventured forth.
You turned and looked upon the gentle hare,
That sat with ears erect and watched us from the field,
You loved, and loved all living things,
Ungracious I, and happy, gambolling hare.

We walked through whitened stubble
To where the way was swallowed by the wood.
Upward we climbed through maze of beeches, oaks and thorns,
Scattering last autumn's smittened leaves;
As through the wood of desolation,
And up the hill of penitence,
Spurred on by love's encouragement,
Unspoke but felt.

We climbed towards the light,
And, breaking from the dark-knit grove,
Gained the summit. There beyond,
The world lay spread in beauty.
Then on and down and over hill and dale we went,
Joyously outfacing chilly wind,
Speaking of this and that,
Of how today stood out a precious day,
Itself a gift, with no claim on the morrow,
And peace was perfect in our hearts.

At journey's end we rested,
Under the trees along the wayside edge;
And, as you smoothed your hair,
That the rude fingers of the wind had roughed,
I looked and loved, and hoped
That I might yet salvation find.

All living and green things that dwell on Sussex earth,
Beneath the kindly sun, bear witness of rebirth.

CALIFORNIA

Waters of Sacramento,
Sun on the Salton Sea,
Groves of orange and lemon,
Desert of Joshua Tree;

Thunderous roar of the rollers
Along the Pacific shore,
Still of the mighty redwoods,
Hush of the forest floor;

Signpost pointing to Lilac,
Road to Mockingbird Hill,
Switchback curve of the mountain,
Smooth as a water-spill;

Flame of the golden poppy,
Struck from the tinder turf,
Ranks of nodding pistons,
Prizing oil from the earth;

Antennae in Mojave,
Reaching for the moon,
Probing eye of Palomar,
To galaxies far-strewn;

Call of the gentle turtle,
Whine of the streaming jet,
Glitter and gleam of the boulevards,
Hollywood, Vine and Sunset;

Magic of film and cathode,
Power of image and sound,
Stirring the minds of millions,
On a screen with a plastic surround;

These are yours,
O California, the golden.

Add the image of Spain to these,
Of the priests and conquistadors,
And of the hardy frontiersmen,
Who peopled the vast outdoors;

And of the modern frontiersmen,
Coming by auto and air,
A hundred and twenty-two an hour,
Lickety-spit they tear,
Seeking the land of golden dreams
And a paradise rich and fair.

But here, of a sudden, the frontier ends,
And the trail is seen no more,
As the mirage of paradise dissolves
In the mists of the ocean shore;
And scarcely a voice is raised to warn,
In this shrine of the media djinn,
That paradise lies in the human heart
And gold is found within.

But California, O California,
You have that gold to give.

STRANGER RAIN

Thirst-quenching rain
Comes splashing down the spout,
Patters leaves,
Beats canvas blind,
And drums the window pane.
Spinning wheels of
Swiftly speeding autos
Hiss the wet streets,
Dark trickles flow
And droplets heavy-hammer on the dust.

Abrupt the termination;
With air clean-washed,
Sage and canyon walls
Don a momentary sheen,
And desert wastes a flash of flowers –
Small suns of orange red and white –
Brave-faced towards the morning sun,
Whose canopy of oven-heat
Settles upon the ground,
And in slow furnace desiccates
These blossoms lately freed from prison seeds;
Now, so soon, to prison seeds returned,
To lie inert, a year or maybe more,
Until, stranger rain returns,
Bearing the quickening moisture from the sea.

HOLLYWOOD NOCTURNE

I, Bill Schultz, movie-cutter,
As I sat by a tree
In Elysian Park
In the cool of the evening
The day we started work
On the four million smacker smash-hit,
"Love Before Breakfast",
I thought as I sat:

'We traffic in men's lives,
We play the passions,
Manipulating hearts
To ring the dollar gong,
When men and women yearn for hope,
Sitting in darkened nickelodeons
In Moscow, Paris and Saigon,
In Sydney and Calcutta,
In Cairo, Rome and Tel Aviv,
In Berkeley and Recife,
And Nashville, Tennessee.'

Then I dreamed:
In every city, as the last reel ended,
As the people stumbled, blinking and bemused,
Into the brightness of the street,
Suddenly a massive light pierced the air.
A vast projection that held a picture
Across the curtain of the sky;
The air about it sparkled with a myriad particles,
As if from giant arcs perpetually renewed –
A motion picture such as we had never seen.
What it portrayed I have no recollection,
But I saw the world halt in its tracks.
Men laughed and sang for joy when they beheld it.
Women forgot to preen and pout.

I saw the man of fear lift up his head,
The gall drain from the bitter man,
The man in money's grip relax,
Become a man once more,
And cold hearts warm again.

This was the dream I dreamed,
Bill Schultz, movie-cutter,
As I sat by the tree in Elysian Park,
In the cool of the evening,
The day we began,
The four million smacker, smash-hit,
"Love before Breakfast".

DOWN TOWN LOS ANGELES

Around me concrete blocks,
And whirling freeways,
Automobiles, palms
And pepper trees,
And wail of ambulances;
And so I long for these:

Warm sun on mellow walls,
And hollyhocks' profusion,
Paved paths of lavender,
Dark-glowing climbing rose,
Rain of bright laburnum;
Daisies cut for Michaelmas,
Red chrysanthenums,
Onions, potatoes,
Cool mint and fresh green peas,
Smooth-polished, shining conkers
Winging pheasant's whirr,
Hop-rabbit by the spinney;
Green cress afloat the stream,
Avenues of mighty beech;
Tall, waving grasses,
White windflowers, harebells blue,
Clover, Tom Thumb and vetch;
Primroses in early spring,
Violet's purple glow,
Bluebell mist, and lilies pale,
Hid deep within the woods;
Hum of bees in sycamores,
Jackdaw's nest in hollow elm;
Wave upon wave of wheat,
Ripe brown hazels ready-wrapped,
Rowan berries gleaming;
Still moon above the pine tops,
That creak beneath the wind,
The lark for ever rising;
So the endless images come crowding
Of beloved Bourton, nestling warmly
On its Cotswold ridge.

THOUGHTS OF AFRICA

By the shores of Lake Huron

I hear the sigh of the forest leaves,
As the dawn wind dips to the shore,
Rippling Huron's shimmering sea,
In a moonbeam causeway beckoning north
To the uttermost rim of earth and sky,
Where Canada lies;

Then northward still to the silent snows,
Up and over the Pole, and down
Through the Nordic lands to the tropic south,
Where the burning heart of Africa
Yearns to find true freedom on earth.

I hear in the sound of the sighing wind
The ache of centuries past,
A yearning that even in this late hour
The hearts of Africa may forge
Freedom for all mankind.

THE PRESENCE

The tumbled rocks, inert, imponderable,
Stretch from the azure bay
Towards a farm and fields of green.
Aloft, a single cloud
Rides white, serene.

Beyond the distant farm a windmill stands
With arms outstretched
To gather power, as they revolve,
From where the winds
Of God evolve.

The scene is filled with great immutables,
Sea, wind and solid rock,
Over which an all pervading
Presence seeks unseen
Hearts that listen and respond.

Porth Hellick,
Isles of Scilly

INSTRUMENTS

We use the hammer, chisel, plane,
Bucket-grab and byte ,
Computer, camera, brush and pen,
And spacial satellite.

We also have the human brain,
Beautifully made,
With which to plan, create and build,
Communicate and trade.

Beyond that brain a fifth sense lies,
But used by very few,
A sensor beamed terrestrially,
With tuning fine and true;

Reaching beyond the bounds of space,
Far from man's domain,
It links with heaven's signals,
And even mightier brain.

Thus can the Spirit permeate,
Enabling human skill
To move in realms miraculous
Through dedicated will,

Receptive to the pulses
Of a power above mankind,
Transmitting in expanding arcs,
The wisdom of God's mind.

EARLY MORNING IN HYDE PARK

London

Sun's crimson disc
Suspended in the curtains of the morning,
Glows through the winter trees
As on a painted backdrop,
Wondrously contrived,
Against which to present
The convoluted dramas of the day:
Tales of toil, mingled fears and joys,
Highest hopes and dreams ethereal,
Some too bizarre to find reality,
Some bold yet simple,
Destined to bring
Overwhelming joy and happiness.

INSTANT OF SPRING

Marlow

Thames, silent, swift,
In level mass,
Slides between shores,

Bearing white tufts,
Of melting snow,
Two months in ice;

Ducks from mud banks
Skitter away
And skyward lift;

Aloft, a plane,
Flashing fish-like
In the warming sun.

Sudden the ridge
Is lipped by
Orb emergent;

Earth leaps in Joy,
And lark soars up
In heavenly song.

EASTER

Pale primroses as heralds come
Before the orchard blossoms' birth,
Spring hurries on its joyful way,
Life permeates the sleeping earth.

At such an Easter time as this,
The Son of God was crucified.
Men hung him from a rough-hewn tree,
His name and calling villified.

High on a hill, hate murdered love,
(While spring imbued each living thing),
And sought to quench the spirit that
Had made the hearts of men to sing.

The primroses now flower again,
Upon the green and timeless hills,
While we yet crucify that love
Persistent in our stubborn wills.

Judas, Pilate, Caiaphas
Cannot alone be held to blame.
We who today shun truth for lies,
Might we not then have done the same?

Yet shame to joy, yet death to life,
Are transformed as is wintertide
Into a new and radiant spring,
In hearts where self is crucified.

JULY BOUNTY

Woodend Lane

Twelve wild strawberries, a pendant of cherries,
A fistful of filberts, and wild hop-flowers,
Pyramids of willow-herb flowing down a hillside,
Snap-dragon, fox-glove, campanula and thyme –

All these greeted me along the verdant lane,
Through the climbing woodlands, on the pastured hills,
Gladdening the heart that I was country-bred
Able still to recognise old friends of childhood days.

APPROACH OF WINTER

Yellow leaves upon the grass,
Still and undisturbed,
A fallen host upon a field of green,
So still, so pale;

From the bough another slips,
Turning slowly, falls;
Then another, spinning, frantically.
Both silent lie.

Soon the mist and rain will come,
Then frost and snow
To wrap the mountain huts in winter sleep,
So pure, so still.

VISION OF YELLOW-GOLD

From head to foot
Aglow in yellow-gold,
Within the darkened room,
As if with sun-fire
Captured from the street without,
(Or maybe from an inner kindling) –
A simple harmony,
Delicate as petals of a rose,
Fair hair, sweet lips,
And flowing dress of yellow-gold.

TO BE

For a friend, facing the future

Scan the four winds,
Flash thoughts across the oceans,
Europe, Africa, and Asia,
Imagination encompassing the world.

Boundless future extends eternally,
Packed with fabulous adventure,
Richest dreams and treasures of the heart.
We penetrate the secret spirit realms,
Explorers of a golden way,
Treading where but few have gone before.

All joys compressed
In one were nothing then.
Dare but walk with destiny,
And follow where your calling bids you go.

Homemaker true,
Bearer of grace and peace,
That heals, inspires and frees cold hearts.
Which in their turn may true fulfilment find.

HOMECOMING

The plighting of a Troth

Soft-carpeted with bracken,
The woodland glade
Lay smiling in the sun,
And all around us sang
The music of the spring.

Here in this greenleaf bower
We spoke our hearts,
Without demand, with nothing hid,
And love was free to give.

Then the hurts and fears
Were washed away
As by a swift and crystal stream,
And we were one;

Then instantly were headlong swept
Towards the shores of paradise,
Overwhelmed by God's amazing,
Boundless grace.

DELIGHT

Beyond the long expanse of grassy green,
We saw the white Pavilion of Delight,
Elegant and sparkling in the sun,
Like some enormous crown among the trees.
A scene of scintillating beauty
That made the heart leap up in purest joy.

When we had crossed the grassy lawn
We came into the magic, arched octagonal,
A fairy gondola it seemed,
Floating high above the earth.
For here, we were upon a hill-top edge,
And, gazing out on vistas far below
Of lake and wood and gentle curving slopes,
It seemed the gondola invited us
To soar aloft for ever and a day.

It was a vision of eternity,
And in that fleeting moment came the flash
Of promises of even richer joys,
Those joys not only of the human eye,
But of the deepest feelings of the heart.

Claremont,
Surrey

TASKS COMPLETED

How often in these years
Have we been borne on waves of surging hope,
And from these crests have glimpsed the distant shore,
Then downward plunged in troughs of further toil.
Yet still the breakers bore us to our goal,
Where rest and sweet fulfilment seemed to wait.

But inactivity has never been our bent,
With other tides to ride and shores to gain,
Midst hazards, challenges and tests of faith,
Perhaps the intentioned pattern of our lives;
If so, then let us contemplate and weigh
The total sum of joy in tasks fulfilled,
Rejoicing in the gifts we have received,
And wondrous visions set before our eyes.

NOTES

Page 7. *Journey North*: Shap Fall is a mountain pass in the north Pennines, not far from Penrith. It is one of the main routes to Scotland, and through it run a major highway and a mainline railway.

Page 9. *Sheffield Steel*: In the 1950s this was a flourishing, major industry, renowned world-wide. There also existed a widespread, radical and revolutionary spirit in the industry, especially in some of the trade unions.

Page 10. *The Valley of The Windrush*: Naunton is a village of the North Cotswolds, not far from Stow-in-the-Wold. The Windrush rises in the upland village of Cutsdean, flows down through Temple Guiting and then along the narrow valley where Naunton lies. It continues on through Bourton-on-the-Water, Burford, Minster Lovell, and finally joins the Thames at Newbridge. Thus it's waters, mingling with the greater river, finally flow through London and beyond it to the North Sea.

Page 13. *June Rain*: Longborough is on the eastern slope of the Cotswolds, between Bourton-on-the-Hill and Stow-on-the-Wold, where it overlooks the Valley of the Evenlode.

Page 15. *Summertime at Bourton*: Bourton-on-the-Hill, in contrast to its namesake-neighbour Bourton-on-the-Water, clings to a steep Cotswold hillside, where red valerian and mauve aubretia drape cottage garden walls fronting the road. For many years it was a closely-knit community of farmers, farmworkers and stonemasons, and had its own postman, baker, blacksmith, village store-cum-post office, school-teacher, grand lady with a Daimler, and a taxi-driver who was the proud owner of a black model-T Ford open tourer.

Page 18 *Shakespeare's Avon*: The many-arched bridge at Stratford-upon-Avon was built by Sir Hugh Clopton in the 15th century. It lies only a short distance from the street where Shakespeare was born and grew up, and would have been a familiar sight to him. Caroline Spurgeon, the Cambridge Shakespearean scholar, in her book, *Shakespeare's Imagery*, writes of looking down from the arch on the right and observing the swirling eddies that produce a movement against the current, and suggests that Shakespeare must have had this in mind when he wrote the lines 1667-1673 describing Tarquin's anguish in the poem *The Rape of Lucrece.*

Page 20. *Exmoor*: Oare is the village immortalised by R. D. Blackmore in his romantic novel, *Lorna Doone.*

Page 27. *On crossing Brunel's Bridge*: The bridge at Saltash over the estuary of the River Tamar was built in 1859 by the engineer Isambard K.Brunel. It carries the main railway running westward from London into Cornwall. The original structure still stands and escaped the mass bombing attack that destroyed much of nearby Plymouth in World War II.

Page 29. *London Under Threat*: By June 1940, the tide of war was nearing the Channel coast and Britain was threatened with invasion and heavy, aerial bombardment.

Page 30. *Air Raid on Good Friday*: During World War II, London's ground defences against bombing attacks included ground batteries of anti-aircraft guns. Among them were those an Hampstead Heath and in Hyde Park, the latter being within central London. The poem was written within a mile of Hyde Park.

Page 31. *Tom Shillington*: A graduate of Trinity College, Dublin, he worked in central London during the late 1930s. Until he was called into the armed forces he was active in the civil defence of London, and organised and led fireguards in his particular sector. Enlisted in the Royal Tank Corps, he was posted to the North African desert. During the El Alamein battle with Rommel's forces, one of his tank crew was wounded. Leaving the safety of the tank turret he went to the aid of his comrade. But he himself was hit and killed.

Page 33. *Into Europe*: Following the liberation of France in August 1945, civil communications between Britain and France were soon restored. Trains began leaving the French ports for the heart of France and beyond. This picture shows the Paris Express about to leave Calais in the evening sun of July 1946.

Page 34. *House upon the Mountain*: In May 1946, two Swiss citizens, an engineer and a diplomat, supported by donations from all over Switzerland, purchased a derelict, former luxury hotel half way up a mountain, which had housed wartime refugees. These Swiss citizens were fired with a vision. It was that this building could become a centre for the uniting and healing of a bruised and divided Europe. With the backing of like-minded people, they renovated the building with voluntary help. In July 1946, it re-opened its doors. Since then, the world has crossed its threshold. It has become a magnet for thousands seeking the key to revolutionary change in the human element that underlies so many of the pressing, global problems.

Page 40. *California*: Gold was discovered in the Sacramento River of California in 1848, and later on, to the south, oil also. By the 1960s, in what was a fruit-growing valley there developed the world's largest film production industry, and subsequently a vast electronics industry. The once empty Mojave Desert now not only welcomes tourists but is involved in major space research.

Page 42. *Stranger Rain*: Rain clouds, sweeping in from the Pacific Ocean, release their moisture on the coastal ranges and the easterly Sierra Nevada Mountains, and sometimes on the desert areas. In the spring, this rain, when it falls an parched ground, awakens dormant seeds and produces a brilliant carpet of wild flowers. The picture shows Desert Primroses, the Prince's Plume Lily, and behind them, Fremont's Buttons.

Page 44. *Hollywood Nocturne*: Elysian is a tree-shaded, public park, between Hollywood and down-town Los Angeles. A movie cutter is a film editor.

Page 47. Thoughts of Africa: The northern tip of Michigan's Lake Huron is the meeting-place of the three Great Lakes – Michigan, Huron and Superior. At this junction lies the Island of Mackinac, a magical place held sacred by generations of true native Americans (the North American Indians). In more recent years it has provided a meeting-place and place of assembly where different nationalities have come together, including many from Africa.

Page 66. *Delight*: The 'Pavilion of Delight' is in the gardens of Claremont, near Esher in Surrey. These were created originally sometime before 1720 by Sir John Vanburgh, architect of the great edifices of Blenheim and Castle Howard. His colleague was Charles Bridgeman. Claremont was later extended by William Kent and 'Capability' Brown. It has always been a place of great serenity. Among those who lived there were Clive of India, Prince Leopold, who became King of Belgium, Queen Victoria during her childhood, and Prince Louis Philippe, the exiled King of France.